Wound from the Mouth of a Wound

Wound from the Mouth of a Wound

POEMS

torrin a. greathouse

MILKWEED EDITIONS

Published 2020 by Milkweed Editions
Cover design by Mary Austin Speaker
Cover art by Cael Lyons

Milkweed Editions, an independent nonprofit publisher, gratefully acknowledges sustaining support from our Board of Directors; the Alan B. Slifka Foundation and its president, Riva Ariella Ritvo-Slifka; the Amazon Literary Partnership; the Ballard Spahr Foundation; *Copper Nickel*; the McKnight Foundation; the National Endowment for the Arts; the National Poetry Series; the Target Foundation; and other generous contributions from foundations, corporations, and individuals. Also, this activity is made possible by the voters of Minnesota through a Minnesota State Arts Board Operating Support grant, thanks to a legislative appropriation from the arts and cultural heritage fund. For a full listing of Milkweed Editions supporters, please visit milkweed.org.

Library of Congress Cataloging-in-Publication Data

Names: Greathouse, Torrin A., author.
Title: Wound from the mouth of a wound : poems / Torrin A. Greathouse.
Description: First edition. | Minneapolis, Minnesota : Milkweed Editions, 2020. | Summary: "Wound from the Mouth of the Wound was selected by Aimee Nezhukumatathil as the winner of the 2020 Ballard Spahr Prize for Poetry"-- Provided by publisher.
Identifiers: LCCN 2020028619 (print) | LCCN 2020028620 (ebook) | ISBN 9781571315274 (paperback ; acid-free paper) | ISBN 9781571317155 (ebook)

Subjects: LCGFT: Poetry.
Classification: LCC PS3607.R42873 W68 2021 (print) | LCC PS3607.R42873 (ebook) | DDC 811/.6--dc23
LC record available at https://lccn.loc.gov/2020028619
LC ebook record available at https://lccn.loc.gov/2020028620

Milkweed Editions is committed to ecological stewardship. We strive to align our book production practices with this principle, and to reduce the impact of our operations in the environment. We are a member of the Green Press Initiative, a nonprofit coalition of publishers, manufacturers, and authors working to protect the world's endangered forests and conserve natural resources.

for my crip kin, my dis' kin,
for my trans siblings & elders,
& all those yet to arrive

CONTENTS

Wound from the
Mouth of a Wound

Medusa with the Head of Perseus

Fiberglass reinforced resin, Luciano Garbati, 2008

1.

I do not want to speak about the beginning
                of this story. Were my scalp a wreath or crown
of mouths, still, I would not open.
                But you already know the myth: rape
that made the body punishment for itself.

2.

Instead begin with the body—itself a kind
                of ending. A new mythology, the severance
of two heads. Where her thighs meet, no
                gash, sex mouthed into injury, no coiled
viper against her groin. Instead, a pale gap
                in stone's imagination—a dream my body
swallows. Each pill, a small cut,
                a slow beheading.

3.

My mother says her first crime was beauty,
                that my father's was how he imagined himself
a god. Call me bloodcurse, fair hair shriveled
                & sprouting teeth, stain across the temple
floor. Do not make me tell this story
                without a forked tongue. Before me
there was a mother & a god—I mean
                a man—& a choice. Imagine, her body a home.
Call my father *burglar*, my birth a *breaking*
                & entering. At least this crime gives a name
to the shatter. Invents a reason for the curse
                birthed into this body.

4.

O, serpent-headed girl, mirror
        that statues its reflection, I blink
& all the stonework shatters.
        I sweep a sea of mirrors into my palm
& suddenly I am wearing my mother's
        face, all these failed children sharpened
into my skin—the bathroom a flood
        of tiny cardinals. Cells that divide & twine
a scarlet thread slithering down my wrist.

5.

My family is the myth of an animal devouring
        itself. What is an ouroboros but a body, or a story,
without a beginning or an end. Medusa braids
        her fingers through her ending's soft brown hair
& takes off his head. A story swallows its first
        words, forgets where it is going. My mother
disowns me & suddenly I am a folktale.
        Am I the serpent-headed girl? Or her endless
reflection? Or the winged mare burst
        forth from her blood? Child of slaughter.
Wound from the mouth of a wound.

6.

I drag the thread of scarlet
        feathers from my palm & watch
my body's unbraiding. How
        a gene, when pulled, unravels a child.
My DNA, a two-tailed snake,
        swallowing my father's face.
I see Perseus's head dangling
        from Medusa's hand & know
transition like this—to hold
        a violent man's face in your hands,
to set him & his blood aside.

I.

i only know how to love the body in [fragments/categories] . . .
i am all of the question marks in your medical books . . .
even in its purest form, the body was still a mistranslation of itself.

—GEORGE ABRAHAM

Phlebotomy, as Told by the Blood

Consider these parallel histories: an emperor once declared war on the sea, sent his men drowning toward victory & the Red Sea is named for the dead algae blooming within it. Can you tell me the difference? Maybe I too am red for all the slaughter carried within me, bastard child of water, lake swelled with rotting fish. What are you searching for when you drag me from you? Your vein a riverbed dredged of impossible children. Cells tested for the echo of your mother's name. Once you were carried in your mother, her belly a lake. If the child before you & all those after sunk, are you the blood or the water? A boat or the first unfinished wolf, wrenching itself from the sea? A bridge too carries bodies & the water carries it. Does this make the bridge a mother or a child? Your mother once told you that if she gave you life she could take it back. Does this make her the bridge or its necklace of nooses? The river or its surface tension? Liquor is lighter than water & so is gasoline. Both burn. Both stained-glass a surface in the sun. Common language says we drown in liquor, perhaps this means your mother is a lake beneath another's surface. What does that make me? A bridge or a glass? Your mother's mother? Sometimes I worry that you've forgotten me. Dry & sober as a boat. Your survival a matter of surface tension. Maybe you believe that you are the bridge, suspended above all your dead. Don't forget, everything erodes. A canyon is just a river's bastard child. Bruise deep in the dirt. All of man's inventions topple, each bridge's arches bullied down to cliché rust. Another history blooming the water red.

Metaphors for My Body on the Examination Table

The wasp burrowed fruit; The hunger
dispossessing where womb could have been; The field
fallow in every season; My stomach,
a mouth; The flood
of rotten teeth; The fearful sweat
of pregnant dream; The woman who never wanted a child
but still weeps at the stillborn of her body;
My mother;
The way that hunger kicks & is a living thing;
The starvation carried in the stomach
like a child; The diagram of the procedure;
The body turned in on itself
like a bloody glove; The pill that births
this body into woman; The pill that murders
the potential of a child; The body hollowed
to a broken vessel; A field salting its own flesh;
The blood, rivered from inside of me
like afterbirth; The chest becoming rose
blossoms, sore as broken dirt; The needle,
dragging me like a cigarette;
The snake choking on its own body; The drowned man's hand
-cuffs; The chrysalis strangling
the moth; The mother of ouroboros giving birth to herself
& herself & herself &; The lie of omission;
A fistful of seeds becoming teeth;
The grandchild never held; The first dead son
my mother does not bury.

Essay Fragment: Medical Model of Disability

The ~~disabled~~ body is always closest   to machine
in its dysfunction.   Most fixable
when it is furthest from human   body
as metaphor/rhetorical question:
If a clock is broken   do you repair it   or
ask the world to conform   to its sense of time.[1]
~~Disabled~~ body as abnormality.   Outlier
that must be removed   from the data
for more *accurate* results.   Medical Model[2] speaks
says people [with disabilities] need to work   harder
to overcome [themselves].   The cure is to make them
more normal.[3]   my ~~disabled~~ body is a price tag
is scalpel bait   a prayer to hospital ceilings
or my ~~disabled~~ body is a weight on society.[4]
The Medical Model says: my ~~disabled~~ body
is like any disease.   If we discover a new & hungry
sickness   is it our duty to cure it   or to let it be?

---

1 You must fix what is holding you back.
2 Formerly *Functional-Limitation Model*; formerly *Biological-Inferiority Model*.
3 Read: less disabled.
4 Another price tag.

When my Doctor First Tells Me I Am a Woman

She doesn't
phrase it this way.   Instead,

asks about my family history
of disease   asks

if I'm still smoking.   Says
a certain kind of incision is hereditary.

Says my breasts are just another place
for sickness   to grow

& I'm reminded of the cyst
in my aunt's chest   my mother's

womb spider-webbed with scar & how
            a doctor refused to remove them.

She says my hormones have reached
biological female levels.

                        & just like that names
woman   the remainder

                                    of my body
when man is stripped away.

As though I will not   someday too
have to convince a doctor of

this body's   malignancies.
Swear this unwanted growth

might kill me   unless removed.
This is how she reminds me

I am the body's closest approximation
a fraction rounded up.   Woman

by inverse proportion.   Last light
passing through the eclipse of a closing eye.

On Examination/Dereliction

My body as radix contritum. My body as transverse fracture. My body as dissection. This waiting room in discount white. This host of bodies, distant in their completion. The slow walk to an examination room disinfected by fluorescence. The echo of my cane. The nurse's eyes on my lips, red as infection. The lemon-sick scent of bleach that cuts through even my bone-choked nose. This baseboard sprouting cracks like roots. Your nurse who calls this body *Sir*. Your doctor who calls it *Ma'am*. Your doctor who mistakes my breathing for sickness. Your doctor who lifts my shirt & loses my spine in the tight mangle of my back. I am always first the crookedness of my body. Before nail polish—calloused palm. Backless dress—a window to the choking of trees. In the cold of the examination room, my fingernails bloom into wisteria. Memory of how slowly, gently, a flower choked my childhood home. How removal could leave the building unable to stand. She prescribes Estradiol, Spironolactone, offers something for the pain. The way my mother whitewashed the porch. How she knew the structure was beyond repair & still insisted on a graceful collapsing.

Hydrocele

There are twenty-two distinct variations of the color white:

mintcream

oldlace   *lavenderblush*

ghostwhite   *ivory*

honeydew

                     & I am trying
         to identify the walls of the emergency room.
   To ignore the cold   snatching at my naked legs.
       Ignore the nurse in between them.

The ultrasound jelly sends false voltage through the swollen part of me.

So soon after I reenter the world,
newborn girl,   I wake in the morning

      cavity of me flooded   testicles a heavy curling fist.
  The way fingernails press into the palm,
          my flesh too rejects the male of me.

The nurse explains this: my body's indecision.
    The mouth of muscle that could have become a doorway
to the womb—failed to close.

      Anatomy begging
       for any part of woman
         to belong to it.

Silently, I praise this body's reluctance   to be named son.

Discovering My Gag Reflex, an Absence

Therapist says I bury
trauma in shock value. No,
that's a lie, therapist is withholding
judgment. This makes one of us.
This story is about sex. But
it's not. But maybe, it'd be easier
that way. His hand clenching like
teeth on the back of my neck. My lips
pressed to the stiff curl of fur. Skin
linoleum white. The story turns
in on itself. Fingers find the back
of a throat, attempt to reframe body
in its emptying. Fail. Saliva curling down
my palm like handwriting. Therapist scrawls
dysphoria in her notes. Saliva pools
with tears on white linoleum. This story
is about sex. But not how you assume
it is. Words load themselves like a gun.
I say gag, you are already imagining
the scent of sweat, the sound of one body
choking on another. Instead I mean
the desperate of one body to empty itself
into change. Instead I mean ketosis, acid
stained teeth. The words do all the work
for me. Reframe the story so it tells itself,
before I even open my mouth.

There's No Word in English for the First Rain of Any Season

My friend's mother used to say
that every time you cry, you are
crying for everything that has
happened since the last time
you cried. Ceramic piggy bank
bursting with a debt of salt.
When I began to transition
it wasn't into a daughter, but
instead a flood. Wide-eyed breach.
Birth of memory. I took the pills
inside me & out spilled blue
nail polish, ropes of silver chain,
my mother's curls, my father's
gin-drowned face, sky blue baby
clothes soaked in lake water, fish
hooks, sapphire earrings, spent
copper shells, Christmas cards,
prom tickets, & my birth certificate
drenched till dissolving, handfuls
of baby teeth, trout scales, burst
ballpoints, vertebrae, knuckle
bones worn to dice, one diamond
missing from a second wedding
ring—the list goes on & on & ends
as all things seem to, polished
brilliant by hard rain.

II.

Elaine Scarry writes that pain is simultaneously
a thing that cannot be confirmed & cannot be denied.

In me, a shooting like a flash like a planet like a fire.
In you, a question mark.

—JILLIAN WEISE

Burning Haibun

Once, my mother accused me of throwing alcohol & gasoline on my emotions. Once, my father's breath was a guilty verdict. His car curved inward like a palm, how it birthed him back as a fist & I became the bloody rise of crescent moons hidden inside. I skin my knuckles & smell the alcohol before it enters the wound. Yesterday, I read that cleaning a cut with this clear burn will worsen the scar, make the undamaged cells forget how to rebuild. Maybe each scar is the skin's blackout. Each blackout, erasure down to the cell. Once, my father tried to collision a child into perfect. Once, I tried to drink myself into blackout or erasure myself into something more poem than memory. Since the birth of words we have languaged our history into burnable things. Papyrus, paper, plastic film. Once, I bought a box of cassettes just to watch their innards burn, flashpoint from wound to wound. Once, the cops accused me of lineage, my blood a guilty verdict, each breath my father's. How we first called *delirium tremens* the blue devils—alcohol possessing the body. How each drink curls me into a tighter fist & this too is not mine or if I claim innocence, each bruised wall, each jaundiced dawn without midnight before it, becomes a guilty verdict. My mother marries an alcoholic & gives birth to kindling. This is to say, my father calls his child a faggot & watches them burn. Did I inherit this addiction from my father or the queer of my blood? Once, I swallowed liquor like guilt & named this family.

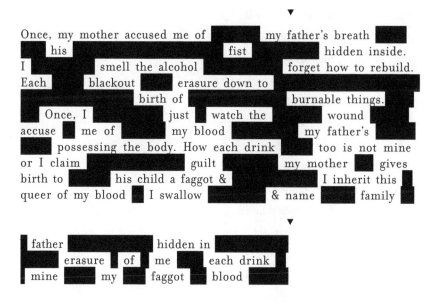

▼

Once, my mother accused me of   my father's breath
      his   fist   hidden inside.
I   smell the alcohol   forget how to rebuild.
Each   blackout   erasure down to
              birth of   burnable things.
      Once, I   just   watch the   wound
accuse   me of   my blood   my father's
          possessing the body. How each drink   too is not mine
or I claim   guilt   my mother   gives
birth to   his child a faggot &   I inherit this
queer of my blood   I swallow   & name   family

▼

father   hidden in
      erasure   of   me   each drink
mine   my   faggot   blood

Ode to the First Time I Wore a Dress & My Mother Did Not Flinch

My palm still recalls the shape, crushed
velvet's soft-jagged pull that makes
my thin jaw ring, my teeth a row
of tiny bells. How it stained my skin's
silhouette the color of a newborn
bruise, before first-puberty made
mayhem of my skin, unbraided
genes to watch their blueprint spill,
moth's unfinished body from split
cocoon. In my mouth boyhood was a fawn,
stomach lined with nettle blooms, a dog
retching grass, bright red of a silver neck
-lace torn from my throat by a boy who bit
small moons from his fingernails
& told me all the ways he could break
my body & no one would even
notice. He left my mouth dry as velvet,
scrubbed from a buck's bone crown, rouge
across a tree's pale face & I loved him
for it. Wanted him to love me back like any
-thing other than a boy. Window. Perfect
pebble. Shooting star. Pen knife. Painted
pair of lips. My mother helped me tighten
the straps, lent me her smallest heels,
& watched me dance with a violent boy's
gentle name on my tongue. I can't
imagine how both of them will see this
velvet slip as nothing more than tender
skin to be shed bloody from a *boy*
to make from him a man.

All I Ever Wanted to Be Was Nothing at All

I was a shrinking child.   Boy born with an apple
     on her head. Flinching target.

     I learned young to be the smallest bullseye.

How a trans girl's body
         is always down range.

     What better way to vanish   than by mastering
       the stomach's calculus.

My ribs the thin slats of an abacus. Each meal
             an equation.

     My mother used to say that if I just   turned
            sideways

I would disappear.

         A trick of the light.
The eye glancing off my body   like an arrow off a blade.

     Woman was taught to me
       in a language of subtraction.

So, I skipped meals.
Trimmed fat.
       Dreamed of another body,   revised
       again & again like the rough draft of a coast.

I was always a mouthful away   from unbecoming.

     Each calorie
     a single match
     struck in the gut.
           I counted sparks.

Factored out hunger's unnecessary variable.

Swallowed an apple
    like a torch. Slice of pizza
        —a wedge of blistering ore. I imagined

myself, a wicker girl   trying not to burn.

        I will not say the word
           scorching both our tongues.

Will not let this become another metaphor

    for how my family taught me
        my body as another name for pyre.

That's So Lame

He says when the bus is late, when the TV
show is canceled, when a fascist is elected,
when the WiFi's bad. *That's so lame!* I say
rubbernecking my own body in the bath
-room mirror. See, every time *lame* comes
out a mouth it doesn't belong in, my cane
hand itches, my bum knee cracks, my tongue's
limp gets worse. Some days it's so bedridden
in the bottom of my jaw, it can't stand up
for itself. Fumbles a *fuck you*, trips over its
own etymology, when all I want to ask is, *Why
do you keep dragging my body into this?* When
I want to ask, *Did you know how this slur
feathered its way into language? By way of lame
duck, whose own wings sever it from the flock
& make it perfect prey.* I want to ask, *How long
have you been naming us by our dead? Baby
-booked your broken from the textbooks of our
anatomy?* A car limped along the freeway,
a child crippled by their mother's baleful stare.
Before I could accept this body's fractures,
I had to unlearn *lame* as the first breath of
lament. I'm still learning not to let a stranger speak
me into a funeral, an elegy in orthodox slang.
My dad used to tell me this old riddle: What
value is there in a lame horse that cannot gallop?

A bullet & whatever a butcher can make of it.

Essay Fragment: Moral Model of Disability

That winter we kept finding the wings
of pigeons pulled from their sockets. Viscera deleted
by the rain. A symbol stripped of its meaning.
Worry bead mistaken for a pebble. My mother
will not admit to our history heirloom of disease.
Once, malformed children were dashed against the rocks
slay the child, spare your now unburdened blood.
My chest is rivered with cracks my sternum broken like
an ox. My father tells me that a wolf will eat
their own young those too weak to survive.
This morning, a stranger in the strip mall offered blessing palms
to pull this shattered bone into church's sharp-edged mercy.
This ~~disabled~~ body is always product or vessel
[of sin/for mercy]. Always this body of crooked back
& sidestepped gender. Body of apple-taker
& rib-giver. This body of ungiftings
worth praying away.

Portland, 1999

Northeast 19th is a powder-stained
July, sky still hot from the glitter
burst of good american fire.
This summer, the hydrants break
like sweat, poverty inventing new magics,
thirsty hands conjuring stolen rain.
On the porch the cat hums like a queen
of spades trapped in tire spokes.
My mother is cracked thumbnails
beheading dead brown blooms.
My father is a palm folding, paper
white fist, an envelope
around the garnet dawn
of my mouth.

Heirloom

My mother bought the plates because they were supposedly
marketed as *unbreakable*. I sweep shards from the floor

while my brother hides in the other room. My teeth cavity
with excuses, with *I don't know my own strength*. But my mother,

she knows how easy ceramic can confetti, shrapnel, warning
-shot, wound. She takes all the proper precautions. I remember

the too-bright paint in the corner of the kitchen wall, the cabinet
of unmatched mugs. I'm misdiagnosed—bipolar this time—then,

three days later, my grandmother is diagnosed with cirrhosis & isn't
this exactly what we mean when we call family by the word *blood*?

I buy two of everything, thick, cheap, & heavy. I don't remember
throwing it. I joke that when I am the last child alive, there will be

nothing left to inherit. My grandmother breaks a wineglass every visit.
Drinks herself to splinters. My mother & I both know the slow ballet

a glass shard makes beneath the skin.

Against Yellow

When I see the child's sky, scrim of blue
crayon, the sun's untidy scrawl, the last thing
I think of is heat & light. Instead, teeth
antiqued by cigarette smoke. Instead, the wash
of bile across the tongue. The honey scent
of ketosis piss, starved body's brightest rebellion.
Instead, my father's eyes. Instead, Van Gogh's
last meal. The color my mother painted
the whole house when my father was drowning
in a bottle, believing instinct would drag him
like any good animal toward the light.
How he once tried to hollow his lungs
into our swimming pool & couldn't stop
his body from surfacing, so he went looking
for a gun instead. I see a child's gentle imitation
of the light & think first of all the rooms
my mother hasn't painted over since he left.

III.

What else could I do?
Nobody *does* childhood;
it just happens to us.

—FRANNY CHOI

In the Dream Where I Wake Up in My Physics Class Naked

The most surprising thing is how, for once,
my naked body is not the most brutal science in the room.

The teacher is giving a lecture on spring mechanics
& all of the softest examples fill his mouth,

> *trampoline,*
>> *pogo stick,*
>>> *pinball machine.*

He asks the class for more examples
& all I can think of is the helix of wire
buried in the cabinet drawer

from when we unloaded
the barrel of my father's

throat, & no one
is answering, so I say

> *a bow & arrow,*
>> *the trigger of a gun,*
>>> *the way skin rebounds*
>>>> *after a father's fist.*

They Leave Nothing for the Morning

I watch from the fence's perimeter,
      two coyotes circling

as they make of their hungers
      a wicked game, a slow dance

of devouring. Between them a bantam hen,
      soft blurt of fear, copper coin

slurring into a planet between four open palms.
      The bird litters a panic

of its blood, ruby crumbs darkening the ground.
      I stand there quiet & do not stop their game.

I am nine & do not yet know this feeling.
      To become a thing of play

& then a meal. But I will learn. A woman
      will howl into me

like the silence of a bell. I will mistake her
      for a teacher. Will awaken

to my skin now a currency I do not hold, sex
      the unwilling barter of a body.

My lips, the tender veins of my neck,
      the delicacy of my tongue,

passed between teeth, from mouth
      to mouth, & I'm taught

to find value in the making of my body
      a meal, in my devouring,

boy broken as bread, or a wishbone's sharp division.
      Then, I was innocent as an animal,

unmarked as a fresh lain egg. Come morning,
      I hose the red away, pluck

feathers like small blooms from the frost
      -choked dirt. Think of the hen,

how it could not have foreseen its own opening,
      its becoming a stain, washed away.

How it first entered into the world, drenched,
      body sticky & golden with light.

Before the Not-Child's Not-Howl

My lover comes inside me
& I weep inconsolable. My body,
pressed almost through the sweat
drenched mattress, impotent as wax
fruit before a starving man.

Outside the window birds pulse
into the air, their wings become broken
scissors etching the clouds
into confetti. Open a doorway
to the sun's soft light & the dark
pit it burns in my eyes—

thin slice of ginger-root, apricot
seed, a stomach's perfect
swell. Every animal sound
reminds me of a future child.
Their ungentle howl. The babble
of a baby's brook-mouth.

After my lover dries the sudden
ocean from my cheeks, I search for beauty
in the world as if I were new.
Gather it in fistfuls. Tongue the sun
-light. Teeth against the buttermilk moon.

My half-sobs syncopated like a heart
not-yet-fully beating. I palm my narrow
hips & imagine a dream passing through
them like wind through the eye of a needle.
Imagine a child, against my chest, still
borne from inside me like a wave.

Imagine my life without this
inconvenient truth: a record rewound
so far it begins with a new song, a choir
of children, mouths curled into the shape
of a grin, a chorus, a laugh,
of a mother's name.

The Queer Trans Girl Writes Her Estranged Mother a Letter
About the Word Faggot & It Is the First Word to Burn

You would figure faggot was a word like a fuse. Easy to trace back to a fire. But, there is no simple history for how this word travelled from tinder to flesh. All I know is, the first time I said it, my tongue burned, & now I'm a wick that's always flaming. Our best guesses lead you back to a woman & witchcraft & unwanted desire. Call a faggot anything that burns. The best daughter I could be was a son. The best son—a mirror burning ants. You taught me the best way to kill something & name it unnature is to set it ablaze. So, I blaze a whole colony—faggots—till it glitters them dead. For years, I hid a box of keepsakes under my bed. It once held a picture of you. But I hold all of the things I love just like you taught me, like a wasp's nest soaked in gasoline. I had a picture of you I loved, then burned. In this way, my memory is a faggot. The last time you had your arms around me, you held me like a match. Our family tree, too, a collection of burnings. The etymology of all my family names leads back to one mouthful of cinders. I say the name you gifted me & it bitters my tongue. I always expected family to be something more like a fuse. As if my blood could trace back to anything as flammable as my skin. You never called me a faggot, but I've learned to spot a fire from the smoke. Sometimes, when you'd click your tongue it sounded like a lighter's wheel. I could practically see the sparks. When you told me I would always be your child, I believed you. I wouldn't understand the brittle hive-paper of my skin or smell the gas on your breath till the Christmas that you kicked me out. That night, I swear that it snowed, or maybe it was just the whole sky full of ash. When you remind me that you will always be my mother, I like to imagine that I wasn't born so much as burst into flame.

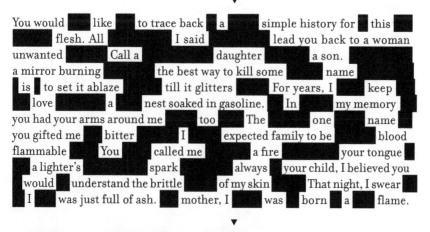

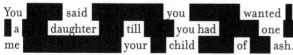

Family Portrait as Unfinished Meal

My mother skins onions
like small game, dabs chemical

tears from the corner of her eye.
The meat tenderizer is broken

-necked, so I must soften
the beef with my father's

hands, marrow-thick
with knowledge

that meat must be beaten
brutal into tenderness.

That any body softens
with violence. She grinds

salt into the carcass like a wound,
a memory. The kitchen sprawls

around our bodies. Open oven
spilling breath into his absence.

I dress the flank with incisions,
fill each new empty.

A palm full of garlic cloves.
A flight of headless doves.

Weeds

The shower stall
my body's confessional
—here, I admit, I love
most what can be
removed from me.

I raise the heat
until my thighs
bloom with small
guilty hands, scrub
dead cells, till
new skin to soil.

Trace fingernails
across my skin, each
red ghost they leave
behind, a scalpel
daydream, plowed
& opened dirt.

False rain feeds a new
season's unexpected
blooms. I have learned
to call them weeds.

Meaning: *unwanted*;
invader; *invasive
species*. I'm taught
removal as "women's
work." Nothing's more
femme than empty

field, a place to bury
seed. I mean, when
my grandfather tells
me, *You will never
be a woman*, this is
a matter of geography,

my body not yet
hollowed. Valley
at the meeting
of my hips, more
forest than clearing.

Pelvis a strangulation
of bloodvine, thick
choke of branches.
I mean, what man
will want to conquer
skin as wilderness
as mine's become?

I mean, this back's
too broken to bend
in all the ways
a woman must.
O, but I have tried

so many methods
to tend this garden
of salted flesh. Gentle
scythe of a razor. Plucked
stems out by their root.

As a little girl, I watched
my grandmother tear
dandelions from the damp
loam & laugh, her breath
winging seeds into the air.

She knelt each day
until the labor curled
her palms inward,
made root balls
of her swollen joints.

Once, I asked her why
she pulled the weeds
each day, only to watch

them return? Why replace
their flower with another
when they are already
there? She told me:

This is women's work,
to remake the wild
into something
a man deems worthy
of keeping alive.

I feel most daughter
when I remember
this, when I make
myself bare despite
the snapped stem,
the split taproot

of me. I first learned
womanhood as
survival—a field,
or body, made
so blank there is no
-thing for a man
to sharpen his
imagination against.

But even when I drenched
the field of my thighs in
a litany of poisons, still
each bud unclenched
its tiny golden fist
as if to say:

We were your first teachers.
Even in the harshest season,
we survive. We bloom forever
where we are told we don't belong.

Hapnophobia or the Fear of Being Touched

After learning that there are over one hundred thirty-two
distinct phobias & still no word for the fear of fishhooks,

I think of my father, his broad hand, unfurled over
my tiny fist, the knife he teaches me to clutch, its rough

handle of recycled bone suddenly gone
slick against my not-yet-calloused palm.

The way the ice box thumps like an unsteady
heart—like I imagine my grandfather's did, that year

in the restaurant, breath snagged sharp in the back of his throat,
face blooded as dawn over his crucifix's pale gold, & we waited

in shock for him to gasp back to his body's surface.
Let me start again, my father dragged the panicked pulse,

a bluegill, out from the ice. Its mouth, like my grandfather's,
a wordless babble. Both their eyes, flat & dull as a copper ashtray.

There is a word for the fear of water, but not of drowning. Another
for the fear of darkness, but not how it hides a person's face.

Sometimes, I forget the difference between an eclipse & silhouette
—sorry, I'm losing the thread—I mean, my father made me hold

the knife. Showed me on the fish where to find an entrance
& make it open. Blade dragged from anus to throat. Its guts

a door kicked in. Its blood escaping like still-hot wind from a kitchen
in the winter where my father told me how, in high school, he wrote

a guide for field dressing humans, *just for fun*. Now, I imagine
every animal he pries open, guts steaming like spring dirt, could be

a child; the scar where I once opened, thin strip of sunset,
that still aches when a lover hooks their fingers to drag

an orgasm's unsteady pulse from inside me, to leave me
gasping, eyes fish-wide & panicked. I mean, some days,

I still can't look straight into the mirror surface of glass
or a fish's eye & there is a name for both these fears.

Like, the fear of dead fish, Ichthyophobia, from the Greek
ichthys, meaning fish, but also the name which Christians used

to hide their faith when it was a hunted thing. Perhaps this makes my fear
a kind of prayer, how some mornings, I wake unable to move, a body

above me, eclipsing the light. Always with a man's face.
& always a gold cross, glitter & flail, strung from his neck,

like a fish with punctured gills, open mouth futile
against the gilded line. Let me start again, once,

my father caught a fishhook through his palm, dipped his hand
into the river & his blood—his blood was touching everything.

Aquagenic Urticaria

I am trying to count the colors blooming in my skin.

My chest a burst of amaranth

breasts blistered into rosebuds

slim hips a garland of cardinals

sutured by their beaks

throat dressed in carmine   & rust.

My doctor calls this genetic condition
          a histamine reaction.   My rabid skin
                    thrashing out its blood
                              rejecting water
                                   like disease.

Like the adobe dirt   desert's hot & blushing flesh
          evaporates the falling drops

makes of them a phantom rain.
A squall of needles.   Severed marionette strings

dancing in the air.

Ekphrasis on My Rapist's Wedding Dress

Still as a scar through the screen's glow, perhaps, this is the origin
of my obsession with the color white. Searching to name this shade.
Color like bitten bedsheets, color like a failed dove, or split lip

when red has ceased howling its way to the surface. Perhaps, the color
of fog over the riverbed that morning, or the color of concrete
that bleach & blood leave behind. It hangs around her like the word

faggot in the air of the locked bedroom. Like drying hemorrhage suspended
between skin & cotton, sideways on the bathroom floor. It hangs around
her like a name that once belonged only to me. & I think maybe

most of all I am jealous. For any metaphor I can put to it, the dress
is still beautiful. Pale & soft & pure. & isn't this just like my poems?
Dressing a violence in something pretty & telling it to dance?

IV.

Thank You doctors and doctors and doctors and every
room I waited in for you I still wait now . . .

—WILLIAM FARGASON

Essay Fragment: Tragedy Model of Disability

Consider: the ~~disabled~~ body   as city.
How its potential   energy [a near-living thing]

cannot be measured   until it is burned.
The body quantified   by the tragedies it can contain.

Consider: after   the [floodwater/sinkhole/firestorm]
the body becomes a sales pitch.   Becomes

a value judgment.   Becomes the price that pity buys.
Reframe the ~~disabled~~ body   as disaster.

The potential energy   between any two molecules is
released   in their breaking.

Like the glimmer of a geode   found only in division.
Patient stone   blistering into light.

Consider the ~~disabled~~ body   the [monetary]
potential   in its rupture.

Our bodies best sold   as aftermath. Each bone
a fault line   spine a mountainside's collapse

cells flooded   with catastrophe.
Consider the price tag   stamped upon the wreckage.

An Ugly Poem

Once, I searched for softness on my tongue, ground
my father's anger, sour mash cavities from my teeth.
I just wanted to talk pretty enough to be mistaken
for what I was. Hot flush of girlish blood. I edited all
my ugly out, made a perfect poem of my soft & lacquered
mouth. Now, I'm looking for the ugly of my tongue,
lolling serpent curled in the slick of my jaw, searching
for its own teeth. I'm a noisy bitch. All *Bark! Snap! Growl!*
My voice still heavy with boy-ghost. Cottonmouth & gun
-powder. My Eve's apple the flint to my blunderbuss
throat. I'm all buckteeth & ulcer, enamel a stained-glass
of nicotine & lip gloss. The brokeback Madonna, arms
tucked around all the empty air I could imagine a child.
Wombless Mary. Patron saint of the ingrown hair,
the bedsore & three-day eyeliner revival. I rise, a slutty
Messiah, from the six-day depression sweat & the good fuck
that ends it. I'm a one-girl armageddon. Nails—cracked.
Polish—chipped. Walk—crooked. Call me *Freakish*
-de-Milo, my body too a crumbling goddess,
stone-cold. This body: holy-trickster. Sacred punchline.
Sometimes, a strange man calls me *BITCH* when I will
not shift for the "big-dick" of his stride & this is a conjuring,
a spell, a blessing. Sometimes, this is the most woman I feel
all day.

Phlebotomy, as Told by the Skin

Before we named the stars, we named the shapes their bodies made.
Sketched legends from the space between the light. Imagined
sparks into monsters & gods. Now, you search for some simple myth
hidden in my fragile skies. The inside of each elbow, needle's soft entry,
punctured into a tiny constellation. Tell me, what faith did you find
in their empty space? Named one arm *Daughter*, the other *Wife*.
Imagine that gender & stretched soft skin are both just boundaries we pass
clean through. & isn't a broken barrier why we're here? Again. Steel
searching for infection buried beneath me. For what some man might have
left behind. Isn't it clever, this medicine of take? The way they draw salt
from inside you, try to find a body & a story in the empty space?
Lost in the constellation of cells. & like any good faith, a constellation is
a map of sorts. See, how you follow it into softness? But there
is always an exchange. The hearts of dying stars reduce to iron.
Their flame the sudden redness of a wound. I mean to say, the cost
of light is hardness. Fire clotting in the distant black. The cost of any
constellation is the iron scars it leaves the sky when—at last—it ceases
to burn. I mean to say, the cost of surviving into softness is this scatter
of dead stars decorating our limbs.

When My Gender is First Named Disorder

Do they mean this as a synonym for *disorganization*?
Machine with excess parts? If I called the parts of me
I no longer want *vestigial* this would imply they were
the vestige of a once-boy. Remnant of a never-was.
Or perhaps they mean it as *disruption* in the neat
arrangement of a system? Misplaced chromosome.
Missing rib. Screw balded as a knuckle. First cell to
metastasize. Our language unable to speak my gender
out of disease. Breasts growing like tumors from a lab
rat's spleen. Cells in *disarray*. Gender as etymology of
abrupted skin. As melanoma severed. The scar a creeping
ulcer leaves. My clutter of apoplectic nerves. Spine a *chaos*
of misplaced bone. Trace vestigial back to its oldest root
& you will find a footprint in the dust. Trace my gender
back to its oldest root & you will find my father's footprint
on my chest, sinking all the way down to my blood.

Still Life with Bedsores

Imagine: the body   a palette
of decay.   Sky stripped
from jaundice to blush to tissue
sloughed away.   Skin cumulus
& beneath it the bone-dull
zenith of the sky.   Gravity coerces
my skin to blossom   fruit   & rot.
Bruise dark & softened flesh.   Plum
plummeting   against cement.
Let every rot be beautiful
as *thrush*.   This infection we name
bird perched   on the tongue.
My hips pulped   by time & gentle
cotton.   The body is a fickle
language.   The way that *rest* means
to lay dormant   but *wrest* means
to tear   away.

Essay Fragment: Preexisting Conditions

It's so simple   really.
A pen invents the anatomy
of a law   & the body
becomes an excuse. Collection of reasons
for its own abandonment.

Becomes diagnosis   checkmarks blooming
across my palms.   Will Saint Thomas
ask to see my hands? The sins
this body carries?   Mother
Mary, scars on my wrists   my spine
a cracked rosary   eyelids a thin & bloody veil.

Trauma repeats in my skull
like supplication.   Fear
becomes a communion
of lightning   on my tongue.

My skull—a panic room
& confessional.   Body named prophet
& whore   faggot   & dyke.
I am damned for the cock & breast of me.
For the split-mind of me.   For the hunger
of my liver.   For the muscle's howl.

I read the list of reasons
I will be left to afford survival
my body's failures cure   on my lips
loose syllables   of a prayer:

Our Father   who forbids us heaven
hallowed be thy name   when the kings
& the bankers count their coins
may they bite for gold
*   & break their teeth.*

Ritual of Small Mercies

I am told I must be kind   to this body of mine.   So, I am practicing
        the smallest mercies.   I oil my hair.   Shave my legs petal-soft.

Shower only long enough   for my skin to rebel   dermis flashbulb red
        rejecting the water   like a spasmed lung.   Massage my breasts

fingers kneading a small   concentric dance   over new-sprouted skin.
        Border eyes   in antimony black.   Contour my cheeks

terraform   a fresh topography of bone.   Invent new methods
        to convince this body   into softness.   Swallow my hormones

red lips pressed   to the wide acreage of my palm.   Peel my mouth away
        & in my hand   a lipstick stain   across the face   of the moon.

Abecedarian Requiring Further Examination
Before a Diagnosis Can Be Determined

Antonym for me a medical
book. Replace all the punctuation—
commas, periods, semicolons—with question marks.
Diagnosis is just apotheosis with sharper
edges. New name for a myth already lived in.
For the sake of *thoroughness*, I have
given until my veins cratered. Tests administered for:
HIV, cirrhosis, glucose, cancer, creatine, albumin, iron, platelets.
I've slept for days, wired to machines. Had my piss filtered for stray proteins
just to be safe. Still, inside my body—
kingdom with poisoned wells. I want anything but an elegy
lining my bones. I just want to be a question this body can answer.
My new doctor writes one referral, then another, still
no guesses. A man in a scowl & lab coat
offers yoga, more painkillers. Suggests
PTSD could be the cause—of chronic pain, my limp, of migraines,
quickened pulse & blood-glittered coughs, of seizures
rattling me inside my skin—O,
syndrome of my perfect & unbroken
transgender arm. They checked my hormones too. Yes.
Unfathomable—a suffering I did not choose. Must be gender, this
vacancy my body makes of its own flesh. How I vanish from myself.
We search for a beginning to this story & find only a history of breakage
x-rays cannot explain. Some girls are not made, but spring from the dirt:
yearling tree already scarred from its branch's severance.
Zygote of red clay that rain washes into a river of blood.

V.

The fall of man was a rib
being torn from a chest
& men calling that violence holy.

—JUSTICE AMEER

Litany of Ordinary Violences

Today, green '96 Subaru, corner of Washington & Alden—six blocks
from my house—a boy punches his car horn & screams wordless
from the window as if to test my fight or flight & which side of that
blade I'll topple from. I keep a list of details & locations in the back
of my head. Red Honda Civic, twelve blocks. Black Grand Cherokee,
half-mile. Yesterday, six drunks followed me into the subway shouting
slurs. Tall blond with tribal tattoos—babyface almost-beautiful
if not for the hunger—his voice the loudest, echoing against the damp
cement & tile: *What the fuck is that thing?* Last week,
a block away from Pride, a street preacher frothed at the jowls
& stuffed my hands with pamphlets describing me hell-bound,
a shirtless man masturbated across from me on the red line,
a commuter in pinstripes & oxfords kicked my cane from beneath
my feet while passing through the fare gates. Each time, I felt lucky.
It could be worse. [I know the difference between *assault* & *battery*—
one violence & another—is proximity to measurable harm. This law
itself another kind of violence, weapon smelted from a certain
bloodline's fear]. The week before, a stranger spat on my feet
on my way to work, another stalked me through the station yelling
Chick dick, chick dick, chick dick, repeating it almost as if it were
a prayer. Today, I slide the dead bolt shut behind me—exhale a breath
I don't remember holding. Tomorrow, who knows? Forgive me.
I cannot find the poem in all of this, but I can't bear to let it go
unspoken. I want to make this violence a stranger in my mouth.
I want to make it something worth remembering.

On Using the Wo|men's Bathroom

I open the door &

step onto cold linoleum	step out of my own skin
wonder who will notice	wonder who will imagine
the stain of stubble	these lips rouged
blued skin & wide-set jaw	by their own rough pulse
ignore the swell of new-	like an eye's own orbit
born breasts & the mechanism	can shadow itself Prussian blue
of these well-trained hips.	beneath a well-trained fist.
Wonder who will see a man	Wonder who will see a man
despite the woman of me	dressed in woman's clothing
& fear my body out of prey.	& decide my body a crime
Make hunger from the implication	himself a fitting punishment.
of each white tooth.	Gender of curled fist
Imagine herself red meat	I am born of abandoning.
my painted face a coyote's skull	I am only ever woman enough
turning in on itself.	to become a guilty victim.

I cannot conceive of a different ending

both doors open   both doors open

to a narrative ending in blood.

Metaphors for My Body, Postmortem

Obituary
of slipped tongues;
A new dress stained darker
than the sky; A toe tag
corrected; The letter *M*
in deep red ink; Mortician's makeup
palette *correcting* the makeup I died in;
Shirt too tight to hide my breasts; Y
incision before chromosome;
A votive candle—face scrubbed
down to glass; A low attended
protest/funeral;
The news report; A *man*
in *woman's* clothing;
The photo album exhumed
& gutted; A mother's favorite
picture of her *son*; A body
buried male; Closed casket;
Endless closet; The grave
—an open mouth
my family lines like teeth;
Another tombstone vandalized;
Another hashtag trending & then

;

Essay Fragment: Economic Model of Disability

How do you calculate   in hard mathematics
the value of a disabled body?   The body which reduces

like a fraction[1]   to an object/icon   of pity?
[In physics] *Work* is defined   as the degree to which

an object[2] is affected   by an applied force[3]
& is not defined by effort   exerted toward a task.

Ex. Two birds   [of equal weight]
fly [at equal velocity]   toward two windows.

If one bird shatters its neck[4]   & one the window
the first bird[5]   has achieved a net work of zero.

Consider the ~~disabled~~ body.[6]   Consider its potential
for work: if *force* is defined [in part] by *mass*[7]

how much weight[8]   can the ~~disabled~~ body exert
[on society]   before the net worth is zero?

---

1 Some portion < human.
2–3 Or body.
4 Spine collapsing like an equation.
5 Still alive, beak loamy with blood.
6 Not unlike the bird—malfunction of anatomy.
7 *F=MA.*
8 Read: burden.

When My Brother Makes a Joke About Trans Panic

It will record   scratch, replay in my mind
that he frames this like advice. This joke

a gutting, a taxidermy of my fear. When I tell him
I am afraid to live in Texas & he laughs

tells me   *You have nothing to be afraid of*
so long as you don't lie about being a woman.

& this is the truth, alchemy of my body
becoming first deception, then a heinous crime.

& then I remember   that Texas still carries
the death penalty, like a proud flag. So, my death

becomes a kind of execution, punishment to match
the crime of transformation. I wonder what the method

will be: skull cracked against the wall, throat wrapped
in a necklace of rope, beaten until my body is no longer

my own, another kind of transformation, my drowned
face floating in the toilet's stale water. I cannot see this

as just a joke   not from the boy who still calls me
brother. Who could read my obituary out loud

& still hear a punchline.

The Body of a Girl Lies on the Asphalt Like the Body of a Girl

    & this does not bear comparison. The body of a girl lies
    on the asphalt & it is not like the splayed anatomy

    of broken fruit. Is not like a gaped wide mouth, throat
    a stoppered bottle. Is not like the mystery of bird

    -less feathers. Or the dull-eyed glint of a wishing well
    gone suddenly dry, down payments on possibility

    parching in the sun. Is not like a bent hammered nail,
    or snapped bough, or the silence after a question's heft.

    The body of a girl lies on the asphalt like only the body
    of a girl, & still someone will name her a man. No.

    Perhaps, the body of a girl lies on the asphalt like
    a daughter. Yes. Just like that.

POSTSCRIPT

Ars Poetica
or

Sonnet to Be Written Across My Chest & Read in a Mirror,
Beginning with a Line from Kimiko Hahn

I could not return to the body that
contained only the literal world: here,

where I cannot say reflect & not suggest
a bending back. Where back does not suggest

the fractured glass of me. I am told to
sever, with a pencil's blade, the word body.

Taught that it does not belong, taught to cut
it away. But look, here it is, real

& irrefutable. Beneath the sonnet's
dark calligraphy, what cannot be spoken

with a psalm-less tongue, music unhinged
from inside a gaping mouth, a body—mine.

& at last a poem that can't be read without
it: crippled, trans, woman, & still   alive.

NOTES

The epigraph for section one is drawn from George Abraham's poem "binary" from their book *Birthright* (Button Poetry, 2020), as first published in *Kweli*.

"Phlebotomy, as Told by the Blood" and "Phlebotomy, as Told by the Skin" owe their existence to Ilyus Evander.

"Metaphors for My Body on the Examination Table" and "Metaphors for My Body, Postmortem" are after George Abraham.

"On Examination/Dereliction" is after Erika Meitner.

The epigraph for section two is drawn from Jillian Weise's "The Body in Pain" from her book *The Amputee's Guide to Sex* (Soft Skull Press, 2017).

The epigraph for section three is drawn from the second installment of Periodic, Franny Choi's column for *Frontier Poetry*.

"They Leave Nothing for the Morning" is titled after a section of the verse Zephaniah 3:3 from the *New American Standard Bible*.

"Weeds" is after Liv Mammone.

"Before the Not-Child's Not-Howl" owes its existence to Siaara Freeman.

"Hapnophobia or the Fear of Being Touched" is after John Murillo.

The epigraph for section four is drawn from William Fargason's poem "Upon Receiving My Inheritance" from his book *Love Song to the Demon-Possessed Pigs of Gadara* (University of Iowa Press, 2020).

"Essay Fragment: Preexisting Conditions" was written in reaction to the list of fifty preexisting conditions included in the text of the 2017 American Health Care Act, which would allow insurance companies to charge customers a higher premium, a practice explicitly banned under the Affordable Care Act that the ACHA sought to replace.

"Abecedarian Requiring Further Examination Before a Diagnosis Can Be Determined" is after Natalie Diaz.

The epigraph for section four is drawn from Justice Ameer's "(After God Herself)" published in *Poetry Magazine*.

"The Body of a Girl Lies on the Asphalt Like the Body of a Girl" draws its title from a line in the Ilya Kaminsky poem "That Map of Bone and Opened Valves."

"Ars Poetica *or* Sonnet to Be Written Across My Chest & Read in a Mirror, Beginning with a Line from Kimiko Hahn" is written in opposition of Michael Ryan and all other poets, educators, critics, and editors who believe that neither the form of a poem, nor the identities of its author, are relevant to the reading of that work.

ACKNOWLEDGMENTS

Many thanks to the editors and staff of the following journals in which these poems first appeared, sometimes in earlier forms and with different titles:

AGNI—"Essay Fragment: Moral Model of Disability"

Anomaly—"Discovering My Gag Reflex, an Absence"

BOAAT—"Ekphrasis on My Rapist's Wedding Dress"

Duende—"On Examination/Dereliction"

Foglifter—"All I Ever Wanted to Be Was Nothing at All" and "The Queer Trans Girl Writes Her Estranged Mother a Letter About the Word Faggot & It Is the First Word to Burn"

F(r)iction—"Family Portrait as Unfinished Meal"

Frontier Poetry—"Burning Haibun"

Hunger Mountain—"Portland, 1999"

The Indianapolis Review—"That's So Lame" and "When My Gender is First Named Disorder"

The Kenyon Review—"Against Yellow," "The Body of a Girl Lies on the Asphalt Like the Body of a Girl," and "Ars Poetica or Sonnet to Be Written Across My Chest & Read in a Mirror, Beginning with a Line from Kimiko Hahn"

The Los Angeles Review—"Before the Not-Child's Not-Howl"

The Matador Review—"When My Brother Makes a Joke About Trans Panic"

Michigan Quarterly Review—"Essay Fragment: Tragedy Model of Disability"

Naugatuck River Review—"Ode to the First Time I Wore a Dress & My Mother Did Not Flinch"

Palette Poetry—"Hapnophobia or the Fear of Being Touched"

The Penn Review—"Heirloom"

Poetry Magazine—"Medusa with the Head of Perseus," "Abecedarian Requiring Further Examination Before a Diagnosis Can Be Determined," and "Litany of Ordinary Violences"

Poem-a-Day—"Phlebotomy, as Told by the Blood"

Poets Reading the News—"Essay Fragment: Preexisting Conditions"

Rascal Journal—"Weeds" and "There's No Word in English for the First Rain of Any Season"

Redivider—"In the Dream Where I Wake Up in My Physics Class Naked"
Split Lip Magazine—"Hydrocele" and "Aquagenic Urticaria"
The Texas Review—"Metaphors for My Body on the Examination Table" and "On Using
     the Wo|men's Bathroom"
Third Point Press—"Essay Fragment: Medical Model of Disability" and "Essay Fragment:
     Economic Model of Disability"
Washington Square Review—"An Ugly Poem"
Waxwing—"They Leave Nothing for the Morning"

"In the Dream Where I Wake Up in My Physics Class Naked" and "When My Brother
Makes a Joke About Trans Panic" also previously appeared in the chapbook *boy/girl/
ghost* (TAR Chapbook Series, 2018).

Immense gratitude to Aimee Nezhukumatathil for seeing the possibility this book held,
the entire team at Milkweed Editions for helping bring it into the world, and to Mary
and Cael for making it far more beautiful than I could have ever imagined.

For all your inspiration, guidance, and care toward this work, my entire heart to: Kaveh
Akbar, Justice Ameer, Kay Ulanday Barrett, Jennifer Bartlett, Billy-Ray Belcourt,
Dan "Soupy" Campbell, Victoria Chang, Meg Day, Natalie Diaz, Ilyus Evander, Siaara
Freeman, Amy Gerstler, Laura Jane Grace, Syan Jay, Sara Eliza Johnson, Cyrée Jarelle
Johnson, Ilya Kaminsky, Ricky Laurentiis, Liv Mammone, Rachel McKibbens, Li-Young
Lee, Sam Rush, sam sax, Danez Smith, Christopher Soto, Brian Teare, TC Tolbert,
Chrysanthemum Tran, Jeanann Verlee, Ocean Vuong, and Jillian Weise.

For the Boston Poetry Slam—my temporary home. And for the Cantab Lounge, now closed,
the walls that held us. I miss you all. May the next place I call home with you have a ramp.

Kit, thank you for all the joys you brought to my life in Boston, and for helping me paper
my walls with this book in its first true physical form.

Nicole, thank you for weathering. For caring for me, and my poems, in every form we've
taken.

Tarik, Julian, George. You are my first message in celebration, in mourning, in humor,
in rage. My dear, petty, petty friends. Without you, I would have given up.

To all my chosen family not named here. You know who you are. I love you.

Раз, ты моя Полярная звезда. Ты—мой маяк. Ты делаешь весь мой мир ярче.

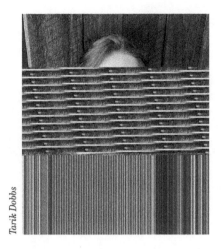

Tarik Dobbs

torrin a. greathouse is a transgender cripple-punk and MFA candidate at the University of Minnesota. She is the author of *boy/girl/ghost* and assistant editor of *The Shallow Ends*. In 2020, they received fellowships from Zoeglossia, the Effing Foundation, and the University of Arizona Poetry Center. Her work is published in *Poetry*, *Ploughshares*, *TriQuarterly*, and the *Kenyon Review*.

The ninth award of

THE BALLARD SPAHR PRIZE FOR POETRY

is presented to

torrin a. greathouse

by

MILKWEED EDITIONS

and

THE BALLARD SPAHR FOUNDATION

First established in 2011 as the Lindquist & Vennum Prize for Poetry, the annual Ballard Spahr Prize for Poetry awards $10,000 and publication by Milkweed Editions to a poet residing in Minnesota, Iowa, Michigan, North Dakota, South Dakota, or Wisconsin. Finalists are selected from among all entrants by the editors of Milkweed Editions. The winning collection is selected annually by an independent judge. The 2020 Ballard Spahr Prize for Poetry was judged by Aimee Nezhukumatathil.

Milkweed Editions is one of the nation's leading independent publishers, with a mission to identify, nurture, and publish transformative literature, and build an engaged community around it. The Ballard Spahr Foundation was established by the national law firm of Ballard Sphar, LLC, and is a donor-advised fund of The Minneapolis Foundation.

milkweed
editions

Founded as a nonprofit organization in 1980, Milkweed Editions
is an independent publisher. Our mission is to identify, nurture and publish
transformative literature, and build an engaged community around it.

Milkweed Editions is based in Bde Ota (Minneapolis) within Mni Sota Makoče, the
traditional homeland of the Dakota people. Residing here since time immemorial,
Dakota people still call Mni Sota Makoče home, with four federally recognized Dakota
nations and many more Dakota people residing in what is now the state of Minnesota.
Due to continued legacies of colonization, genocide, and forced removal, generations
of Dakota people remain disenfranchised from their traditional homeland. Presently,
Mni Sota Makoče has become a refuge and home for many Indigenous nations and
peoples, including seven federally recognized Ojibwe nations. We humbly encourage
readers to reflect upon the historical legacies held in the lands they occupy.

milkweed.org

Interior design & typesetting by Lee Fukui and Mauna Eichner
Typeset in Filosofia

Filosofia was designed by Zuzana Licko for Emigre in 1996
as a contemporary interpretation of Bodoni.

Printed in the USA
CPSIA information can be obtained
at www.ICGtesting.com
JSHW081926200524
63489JS00003B/150

9 781571 315274